The W

Tanika Gupta is the auth
Skeleton, a stage adaptation ot Geeta Mehta's *A River Sutra* and *Flesh and Blood*. Her television work includes the award-winning screenplays *Flight*, *Bideshi* and *The Rhythm of Raz*. She has also written for popular television series and is a regular contributor of original drama for Radio Four and BBC World Service. She is currently Pearson Writer in Residence at the Royal National Theatre.

*Discover the brightest and best in fresh theatre writing
with Faber's new StageScripts*

Sweetheart by Nick Grosso   (0571 17967 3)

Mules by Winsome Pinnock   (0571 19022 7)

The Wolves by Michael Punter   (0571 19302 1)

Gabriel by Moira Buffini   (0571 19327 7)

Skeleton by Tanika Gupta   (0571 19339 0)

The Cub by Stephanie McKnight   (0571 19381 1)

Fair Game by Rebecca Prichard   (0571 19476 1)
(a free adaptation of **Games in the Backyard** by Edna Mazya)

Crazyhorse by Parv Bancil   (0571 19477 x)

Sabina! by Chris Dolan   (0571 19590 3)

I Am Yours by Judith Thompson   (0571 19612 8)

Been So Long by Che Walker   (0571 19650 0)

Yard Gal by Rebecca Prichard   (0571 19591 1)

Sea Urchins by Sharman Macdonald   (0571 19695 0)

Twins by Maureen Lawrence   (0571 20065 6)

Skinned by Abi Morgan   (0571 20007 9)

Real Classy Affair by Nick Grosso   (0571 19592 x)

Down Red Lane by Kate Dean   (0571 20070 2)

Shang-a-Lang by Catherine Johnson   (0571 20077 x)

The Storm by Alexander Ostrovsky
trs. Frank McGuinness   (0571 20004 4)

By Many Wounds by Zinnie Harris   (0571 20097 4)

So Special by Kevin Hood   (0571 20044 3)

The Glory of Living by Rebecca Gilman   (0571 20140 7)

Certain Young Men by Peter Gill   (0571 20191 1)

Paddy Irishman, Paddy Englishman and Paddy . . . ?
by Declan Croghan   (0571 20128 8)

Pelleas and Melisande by Maurice Maeterlinck
trs. Timberlake Wertenbaker   (0571 20201 2)

Martha, Josie and the Chinese Elvis
by Charlotte Jones   (0571 20237 3)

Dogs Barking by Richard Zajdlic   (0571 20006 0)

All That Trouble That We Had by Paul Lucas   (0571 20267 5)

Tanika Gupta
The Waiting Room

ff

faber and faber

First published in 2000
by Faber and Faber Limited
3 Queen Square, London WC1N 3AU

Typeset by Country Setting, Kingsdown, Kent CT14 8ES
Printed in England by Intype London Ltd

A CIP record for this book
is available from the British Library

ISBN 0-571-20514-3

2 4 6 8 10 9 7 5 3 1

*This play is dedicated
to my mother and late father,
Gairika and Tapan Gupta*

The **Waiting Room** opened at the Cottesloe, Royal National Theatre, London, on 25 May 2000. The cast was as follows:

Firoz Raad Rawi
Akash Paul Bazely
Pradip Nadim Sawalha
Priya Shabana Azmi
Tara Lolita Chakrabarti
Dilip Kulvinder Ghir

Director Indhu Rubasingham
Designer Ruari Murchison
Lighting Designer Mark Jonathan
Music Nitin Sawhney
Sound Designer Neil Alexander
Company Voice Work Patsy Rodenburg

Acknowledgements

The author would like to give special thanks to
Lin Coughlan for her guidance and words of wisdom.
She would also like to thank Jack Bradley,
Sue Higginson, Indhu Rubasingham and Paul Sirett
for their encouragement and support.

Characters

Priya
Fifty-three-year-old woman

Dilip
Mid-thirties. 'Immortal soul', in the guise of
the veteran famous Bombay film actor

Akash
Twenty-seven years old. Priya's son

Firoz
Sixty-year-old man

Pradip
Sixty years old. Priya's husband

Tara
Twenty-nine-year-old woman.
Priya's eldest child

Act One

*Set: a lounge with large bay windows at the back which
face out onto a suburban front garden. The walls are
strewn with Indian prints and paintings. There are a few
settees, a book case, crammed with books and photos,
a coffee table, a drinks cabinet and a dining table.*

*As the play opens, it is night, raining, cold and wintry
outside. A strong wind blows in the front garden.*

*In the lounge a body is laid out in a coffin on the
dining table. It is swathed in white sheets and a shroud
covers the face. On the settee we see the shape of a
woman. She seems to be sleeping and is curled up in
a foetal position so that we cannot really see her face.*

*We hear the wailing and crying of several Indian
women – high pitched and feverish. The wailing gets
louder and deafening until three Asian men (Pradip,
Firoz and Akash) enter hurriedly and slam the lounge
door shut behind them, thus blocking out the sound of
wailing. Akash is carrying an armful of bouquets of
flowers. He plonks them all down by the dining table
and then collapses into an armchair whilst Pradip stands
nearby looking lost. Firoz heads for the drinks cabinet
and gets busy with glasses.*

*Firoz is sixty but looks fit and healthy, whilst Pradip is
the same age but looks more bowed. Akash is in his mid
to late twenties.*

Firoz Whiskey?

Akash Please . . .

Firoz Pradip?

Pradip Should I? I mean – is it appropriate?

Firoz Of course it's appropriate. (*He looks at the label on the whiskey bottle and grimaces. Disappointed*) Johnny Walker? Surely you've got something better, Pradip? This stuff tastes like cat's pee.

Pradip Have a look in the drawer, underneath. Priya hid hers there.

Firoz does as he is told and rummages around. He looks pleased with his find and holds up a large, almost full bottle.

Firoz That's more like it! (*Firoz walks over with three glasses and the bottle of whiskey. He places them on the coffee table and pours three large glasses.*)

Akash Firoz Uncle – I thought it was supposed to be against your faith to drink.

Firoz (*amazed*) Have I ever struck you as a religious man?

Akash laughs.

Unbelievable amount of wailing. How on earth do those witches manage to make such a bloody awful racket?

Akash I dunno but I've got a headache.

Firoz Crocodile tears. Did you see your Mira Auntie in the corner? Blubbering like a baby? Everyone knows she disapproved of Priya.

Akash Which one was she?

Firoz The skinny one with the bright orange lipstick.

Akash Oh yeah . . .

Firoz puts a friendly hand on Pradip's arm and gives him the glass of whiskey.

Firoz Drink up Pradip.

Pradip sits down so that he and Firoz are now sitting on either side of the sleeping woman. Pradip slugs back the whiskey. Firoz pours him another one.

When is Tara arriving?

Akash Her flight comes in at seven in the morning.

Firoz D'you want me to pick her up?

Akash No – it's okay, thanks. I think I should be there to meet her.

Firoz Won't you be needed here?

Akash I'll be back in plenty of time – as long as the flight's not delayed.

Beat.

Did you hear what Sanjay Uncle said as he left?

Firoz What's he said this time?

Akash He clutched me to his bosom . . . (*Akash stands and demonstrates.*)

Firoz So you had a full frontal attack of his famous halitosis?

Akash I held my breath . . . I've learnt my lesson over the years . . . anyway he said . . . (*Akash puts on an Indian accent.*) 'Akash, you have been a stranger here too long. Make sure you look after your father.' I said, 'Actually we were thinking of putting him into an old people's home.'

Firoz laughs.

He didn't get it. Then he went – 'Pradip needs something to help him sleep tonight. Talk to Doctor Bannerji. Make sure your father's seduced'.

Pradip (*incredulous*) What?

Akash Didn't dare look him in the face or I'd have cracked up. He said it again – 'If Pradip is *heavily* seduced, he may get some sleep.'

Firoz Idiot.

Akash I kept thinking – I must tell Mum this one. She'll love it.

Pradip Poor old Sanjay. His command of the English language always was a little shaky.

Akash Isn't he a newsreader for the Beeb?

Firoz The Bengali Department, Akash. It's a completely different ball game. He's perfectly proficient in Bengali. It's just the English he has problems with.

Akash (*laughs*) Jambu Uncle came up to me and said he would be very honoured if I would allow him to help in the 'carrying of the coffin' into the service tomorrow.

Firoz But he's a midget with a prosthetic leg. What's he going to do? Hop along the side of it?

Akash Tell me about it.

Firoz It'd look bloody ridiculous. I hope you said 'no'.

Akash How could I?

Firoz Oh God. I can just see it now.

Pradip (*cross*) Will you two just stop it?

Akash (*innocent*) What?

Pradip Have some respect.

Beat.
    The three men fall into silence again. Akash pours himself some more whiskey. He takes a sip and looks angry.

Akash You know when those people came crashing through the door, crying and weeping and gnashing their teeth, I felt so pissed off.

Pradip Your mother was well loved.

Akash I wanted to shout, 'Leave us alone –vultures! She was my mother not yours. What are you looking so bloody upset for?'

Pradip It's their way of showing their grief.

Akash I thought I saw Ma – standing in the hallway. She was smiling at me, looking at me excitedly as if to say, 'What are we celebrating?' Then I lost her in the crowd.

Pradip looks up interested and then stares back at the corpse lying on the table.

Firoz I'm afraid the mind can play cruel tricks and anyway Priya never did like to miss a knees-up.

Akash Yeah.

They fall into silence again. Pradip gets up and wanders out of the room. Firoz and Akash watch him anxiously.

He's not in a good way.

Firoz No . . . well . . .

Akash I've made up the spare room for you. I don't know if I can deal with him on my own.

Firoz Don't worry. I'll be here.

Pradip re enters with a large jug of water. He walks to the drinks cabinet and pulls out a few glasses. Then he starts to pour water into each of them.

Akash What are you doing, Baba?

Pradip For Priya. To quench her thirst.

Akash looks puzzled.

After death, the soul wanders around before going onwards. The soul gets thirsty, so we must make sure she has water.

Akash (*unconvinced*) Right . . .

Pradip wanders around strategically placing the drinks around the room.

Who *were* all those people? Apart from Amit Uncle, there wasn't a single relative amongst them.

Firoz The Bengali community in all its wailing, morbid finery.

Akash They said they all came over on the same boat as Ma.

Firoz That's a lie.

Akash How do you know?

Firoz and Pradip exchange a look.

Pradip Because he came over with her.

Firoz I was sent by your father as her chaperone.

Akash (*laughs*) You?

Pradip looks sadly at Firoz.

Firoz 1968. We set sail from Bombay docks and it took twenty-one days. Aden, Egypt, up through the Suez Canal, Italy, Dover.

Akash I never knew that.

Pradip walks over to the body and stares at it.
The woman who has been asleep on the couch stirs. It is Priya. She sits up and looks around, slightly dazed. Then she notices the half empty bottle of whiskey. (She is dressed in a track suit-type outfit.)

Priya Oy! That's my best malt whiskey you're guzzling down there!

Akash and Firoz don't see her. She waves her hands about in front of their faces but gets no response.

(*to Akash*) Finally honoured us with a visit have you?

Firoz It's funny – she was in such good form last night – wasn't she Pradip?

Priya (*to Firoz*) Hey! Crater face! Inch dick!

She claps her hands to try and get his attention.

Pradip Last night? Was that yesterday?

Priya (*to Firoz*) Don't ignore me.

Firoz Seems like a hundred years ago. (*to Akash*) We all went out for a meal.

Akash Did you?

Firoz I took a cab and she insisted that her and Pradip should walk home. Said it was good for their health.

Akash (*sarcastic*) Evidently.

Firoz Like I said, she was on good form. Wasn't she, Pradip?

Pradip Yes. She was.

Beat.
Akash puts his feet up on the coffee table in front of him.

Priya (*to Akash*) Feet *off* the table please.

Akash keeps his feet on the table. Priya shakes her head. She listens in to the conversation – baffled. Firoz pours Akash some more whiskey.

Pradip Go steady on that. He has to keep his head straight for tomorrow.

Firoz (*gently*) Akash. It's going to be hard on you.

Pradip You'll have to put a live burning coal in her mouth – before – the cremation. You must prepare yourself.

Firoz looks away disgusted.
Akash is upset.

Priya Bloody hell, how much of that stuff have you drunk?

Akash I don't see why I have to do it.

Firoz It really is quite a barbaric custom you Hindus have.

Pradip (*annoyed*) It's his duty.

Priya looks more and more confused as she listens to the conversation.

Akash Yeah – but Tara's the oldest.

Pradip (*angry*) But you're the son. You must put fire in your mother's mouth. Set the burning of her body in motion.

Akash Why me? Why not you?

Pradip I can't.

Akash Why?

Pradip Because she was my wife.

Akash Oh – and I don't count?

Pradip It's the way things are done.

Akash It's revolting!

Firoz Come on, you two.

Akash sips some more whiskey angrily. Pradip watches him with pain.

Pradip You have to be strong for me. You have to shoulder some of the burden now. I can't do this on my own.

Akash looks guilty.

Akash Okay, okay.

Priya approaches them anxiously.

Priya Listen – is this some kind of a joke? Because you're really freaking me out now. Okay? Happy? Ha! Ha! Ha! I get it. Now give me a drink and stop being so bloody morbid.

Priya walks over to the shrouded body and peers closely at it. She turns to Pradip.

(*outraged*) Who's the stiff? And what's it doing in my living room?

The stage goes dark and Akash, Pradip and Firoz leave.
  Priya is left on her own. She looks around her, shocked.
  There is a hush as the stage goes dark except where Priya is standing.
  She stands and looks confused and afraid.

Firoz? Pradip! Where . . .?

As the lounge seems to disappear from view, Priya becomes aware of dark shadows creeping around her. She tries to edge away from the shadows but they seem to come closer and closer. She hears a thudding of footsteps and heavy breathing coming towards her. Priya is terrified.

Where am I?

She starts to hear a whispering voice. Priya rushes to the corner and tries to hide – but there is nowhere to hide. She is terrified.

(*calls out*) Help me. Someone . . . help me . . .

The footsteps stop. Priya, who is crouching and quivering in the corner, sees a young strikingly handsome man walk in, in a halo of light (Dilip). He is dressed in a dark western suit in the style and cut of the 1940s. He looks very swish with his overcoat slung across his shoulders and a trilby hat perched on his head. As he takes off his hat we see his hair is slicked back beautifully. Priya seems to recognise him and is agog and excited. She raises herself slowly.

(*incredulous*) It's . . . it's . . . my goodness. You? How?

Dilip (*upper-class Bombay drawl*) Delighted to meet you – Priya Bannerji.

They both do 'namaste'.

Priya You know my name?

Dilip But of course. I have made it my business to know everything about you.

Priya (*laughs*) About me? That's a good one.

Dilip brushes the dust off his coat and looks cool.

I've seen almost all your films. When I was a girl I saw *Andaaz* fifteen times . . . with Nargis . . . oh she was so beautiful. And that song.

Priya sings a verse of the song and laughs.

I am honoured. Dilip Kumar in *my* house. Please sit. Some tea? (*Calls out.*) Pradip! Pradip! You'll never guess who's here? (*She chuckles like a child.*) It'll give him the shock of his life. Of course, he claimed always that he wasn't into Hindi films. But when it came to you – well they don't make them like they used to – eh? (*She laughs. Calls out.*) Akash! Some *mishti*! *Cha*! Sit. Sit.

Dilip I prefer to stand.

Priya Of course, as you wish.

Dilip I don't want to rush you but . . . (*He looks at his watch.*)

Priya Please. Stay for some tea. And you must meet my son – (*Calls out.*) Akash!

Dilip He can't hear you.

Priya He was here a moment ago. Maybe they've all gone upstairs.

Dilip They're not 'upstairs'. More shall we say, geographically located 'downstairs'.

Priya I'm not sure I catch your drift. You know you do look remarkably well.

Dilip The years have been kind.

Priya So well preserved – must be the magic 'potions and lotions', eh?

Dilip (*starts to get down to business*) Priya. Let's not beat around the bush – yaar – My time is precious.

Priya I understand. How can I help you?

Dilip It is *I* who have come to – shall we say instruct *you*. We have certain formalities we have to go through. Certain procedures that we must follow.

Dilip produces a piece of paper from his pocket and runs through it with his finger.

Dilip I like to write these things down so I don't get anything wrong – yaar? Ready?

Priya Ready?

Dilip (*getting formal*) Okay, so, tomorrow's the big day when your body will dissolve. It is, as they say, a shell – so it is of no use to you now. I must warn you that there

will be – how shall I put it? A sudden power surge.
(*Pleased with his description.*) Yes, that's rather good – a
release of energy when your essence is finally drawn out
from your navel.

Then you have three sunrises left to roam the earth.
First you must visit your past, pay homage to this life
then you may talk to your family in their dreams. I will
help you in that department – it's fairly simple.

Then on the fourth sunrise you will depart the earthly
world entirely. You will be free. That is when you and I
will part company and you enter the spirit world. (*Dilip
squints at the piece of paper.*) Ah yes 'The Waiting
Room'. Some call it Paradise, others call it heaven –
whatever.

Priya (*utterly bewildered*) Dilip Sahib. Is this a rehearsal
for a new film?

Dilip looks exasperated.

Dilip Have you been listening to a damn word I've said?

Priya There's no need to be rude.

Dilip Now I've lost my place.

Dilip looks through his notebook.

Dilip Here we are . . . You can choose to be reborn or
stay in the ethereal world until you're ready.

Priya What in buggery are you talking about?

Dilip (*tired*) We are wasting valuable time Priya. You
play games here and it will only mean that the end will
be rushed.

Priya You're the one playing games.

Dilip (*deadpan*) Priya. You're dead. You had a massive
cerebral haemorrhage – a stroke.

Priya laughs.

Priya Do I look dead to you?

*The body on the table lights up slowly. Dilip walks
over and stands by it.*
    Priya approaches it. She is afraid to go close.
    *Priya hesitates and then goes closer. She removes
the shroud and looks at the face. At first she is
stunned and speechless.*

Dilip That's you.What you see there before you is your
body. What you are now is the spirit of what was.

Priya That's absolute rubbish.

Dilip (*amused*) You have a better explanation?

Priya That's not me.

*Priya is still unable to grasp the truth. She walks
round and round the body.*
    Dilip watches her.

Dilip (*gentle*) I'm sorry. I thought you knew. Sometimes
it happens. Souls emerge dazed and confused.

*Dilip puts a comforting hand on Priya's shoulder.
She suddenly gets angry and shakes Dilip's arm off.
She moves away from him.*

Priya So who in buggery are you? Dilip Kumar's not
dead. I saw a film with him in it last week and come to
think of it – he was fat and bloody old.

Dilip Still a good actor though.

Priya The best . . . You think it's a joke to dress up as
one of Bombay's finest?

Beat.

Dilip I am an immortal soul. I guide the dead through
their first steps.

Priya I'm not dead.

Dilip I came as Dilip Kumar because he was your hero. The one person you looked up to and worshipped. I am here to guide, advise and comfort you. Some prefer Buddha, Mohammed, Jesus Christ, Lord Krishna; but you – you called for Dilip Kumar. So . . .

Priya I didn't call for anyone. Least of all you.

Dilip Let us please move on.

Priya No.

Dilip There is nothing to do but accept. If you do not then I'm afraid things could turn out badly. You could end up as one of those earth-bound, lost souls wandering around weeping and moaning. They're very sad creatures.

Priya looks at her body again. She is depressed. Dilip takes off his overcoat and places it neatly over his arm.

Priya (*incredulous*) Are you trying to tell me that's it? End of chapter? I don't get another chance?

Dilip Another chance – yes. With Priya Bannerjee . . . no.

Priya (*explodes*) But that's so unfair. I haven't finished. My daughter's coming back to see me. We're going to India together – for a trip . . . I have plans!

Dilip looks bored, puts on his shades. Priya stays sitting in the lounge.

It is night time. We are back in the lounge. It is still windy and rainy outside.

Priya is standing near the body, looking mournfully at it.

Pradip enters in his dressing gown. He pads around the room, looking for something along the bookcase. Eventually, he finds what he's looking for – a pair of scissors.

He walks over to where the corpse is lying and carefully snips a lock of hair from Priya's head. He strokes the hair lovingly and then delicately wraps it up in some tissue and puts it in his pocket. Priya watches all this with affection.

Then Pradip walks over to the stereo and puts on a CD. It is the Hindi film song Priya was humming earlier on. He sits in an armchair and listens to the song forlornly.

A yawning Akash enters, in a T-shirt and shorts.

Pradip Couldn't sleep.

Akash Me neither.

Akash picks up the whiskey bottle.

Akash Fancy another drop?

Pradip I'd better not.

Akash nods and replaces the whiskey without pouring a drink.

Firoz enters, yawning. He looks surprised to see the other two men. He slumps quietly into an arm chair.

Firoz I heard some music down here so I thought . . . well, better than lying in bed wide-eyed.

Firoz and Akash sit and listen to the song.

Pradip This was her favourite song.

Akash She used to play it enough.

Pradip Drove me mad. I hid it once for three weeks.

Pradip gets up wordlessly and starts to top up the glasses of water he has already put out for Priya. Akash and Firoz exchange a glance.

Firoz If any of that water disappears, we should inform the local Hindu temple committee.

Akash Yeah – they'd probably come and certify this place as a holy shrine.

Pradip gives Akash and Firoz a dirty look. Firoz pulls a face at Akash.

Firoz Pradip, you don't seriously think that Priya's going to drink that water do you?

Pradip You never know.

Firoz looks back at the corpse on the dining table. He sees a face looking in through the bay windows. For a moment he is frozen in horror. The person starts to gently tap on the window.

Firoz (*scared*) Shit.

Akash looks up and follows Firoz's gaze.

Akash Tara!

Pradip looks up. He hurries out to open the door. A few moments later, he re enters with Tara. She is a young Asian woman (twenty-nine) dressed for sunnier climes.

She looks disorientated. Priya looks up from the body, pleased and excited to see Tara.

Pradip You were supposed to be getting here tomorrow.

Tara I managed to get on an earlier flight.

Pradip Why didn't you call us?

Tara I just wanted to get here.

Priya rushes over to Tara.

Priya How was Cairo? You've got a tan. I told you to stay out of the sun – look at you – almost black.

Tara looks at her father and embraces him. Pradip looks close to tears. Akash then goes over to his sister and awkwardly embraces her.
Firoz starts fussing around her, taking her jacket and bag. Everyone is embarrassed and doesn't know what to say.

Tara Firoz Uncle – hi.

Firoz Tara. You know for an awful moment back there – when I saw you at the window – I thought . . . well . . .

Tara turns and looks at her mother's corpse lying on the table.
Tara is emotional. She walks over to the corpse and stares in. The men all look awkward.
Priya stands by Pradip as he is speaking. She watches Tara's reaction.

Pradip We went out for a meal. Me, her, Firoz. She ate well, we walked home and then she complained she had a splitting headache. I gave her some paracetamol – she lay down and went to sleep. I came down to lock up and when I climbed in next to her –

Pradip can't continue. Tara looks at him horrified. Firoz comforts Pradip.

So quick. She was talking to me just ten minutes before.

27

Tara reaches in and touches her mother's face.

Tara She's cold. Who dressed her?

Pradip Mira.

Tara Why is she wearing such a dowdy sari?

Pradip I didn't oversee that part. I simply let Mira deal with it.

Tara Has everyone seen her like this?

Pradip Yes.

Akash Tara – what does it matter?

Tara Trust Mira Auntie to dress her like a beggar.

Tara looks at the three men and shakes her head.
Tara bends over and kisses the face.
Akash looks away.

She was going to take me back to her birthplace in Benares and then we were planning a tour of South India and all the temples.

Pradip She was looking forward to it.

Tara I spoke to her on the phone only last week.

Tara picks up her mother's hand and touches it against her cheek. She starts to sob quietly. The men all look terribly uncomfortable.

It's not fair. She was only fifty-three! Always too busy looking after everyone else.

Tara starts to sob uncontrollably, almost collapsing on the dead body in the coffin.

Ma, Ma . . . I should have been here. I'm so sorry . . .

Priya (*emotional*) It's all right baby – I'm here . . .

Akash moves over to Tara and tries to comfort her.
Pradip looks helpless.

Pradip What good is it if you start crying?

Akash Baba!

Pradip How do you think I feel? I'm the one who's been left behind. I'm the one on my own.

Akash She's upset!

Pradip (*scoffs*) She's upset.

Akash holds on to Tara as she weeps. Pradip, unable to deal with the emotion, exits. Firoz looks at Tara and Akash together and then exits.
Dilip enters and approaches Priya.

Priya (*to Dilip*) Look at her. Such a clever girl. An environmental lawyer – high-powered. Travels all over the world – changes boy-friends like socks. (*to Tara*) Darling, I have my passport sorted. We can go whenever you're ready. I've written to my aunt in Delhi and . . .

Dilip She can't hear you.

Priya ignores Dilip.
Akash tries to pull Tara away.

Akash Come on, you've got to get some sleep.

Tara I want to be near her. I haven't seen her for three months. Just want to look at her face.

Akash What's the point? She's not there.

Priya (*to Tara*) As we agreed, we'll start off in Delhi. Shop 'til we drop. And then head off to Benares . . . I'll show you the little house where I was born.

Dilip Priya . . .

Tara At least I can still see her. Tomorrow, even that will be destroyed.

Akash Almost don't recognise her as Ma.

Priya is getting more desperate.

Priya (*still to Tara*) Just us girls, eh? No men. Get away from this ghastly winter and enjoy the sun on our skins. We'll have such a good time, eh? A trip of a lifetime.

Priya realises that it's all fruitless. She turns away from Tara, upset.

Tara Where were you when it happened?

Akash Baba phoned me on the mobile. I was in the pub. Came straight over. He was in such a state. It was horrible.

Tara You were in the pub?

Akash I didn't know, did I? At least I was in the same country.

Tara What's that supposed to mean?

Akash Nothing, come on, let's not fight. It's late. Get some sleep.

Tara You go.

Tara spots the whiskey on the table, walks over, opens it and takes a slug straight from the bottle. Akash watches her with unease.

Tara None of us were here when she died.

Akash Baba was here.

Tara He left her to lock up. She was on her own.

Akash She went peacefully, in her own house, in her bed.

Tara I never said goodbye.

Akash It doesn't work that way.

Tara (*angry*) Look at her Akash. She's dead. Our mother is lying there, not breathing, swathed in some crappy cotton sari. Don't you feel anything?

Akash (*taken aback*) Why are you having a go at me?

Tara takes another swig from the bottle.

Tara I should have been here. I was coming back to take her away. If she'd just held on a bit longer.

Akash Think you're so special don't you?

Tara We understood each other.

Akash You trying to say I didn't?

Tara Got to eighteen and you couldn't wait to get out of here.

Akash You can talk.

Tara At least I kept in contact.

Akash Did my head in with her nagging. Never stopped.

Tara That's because you deliberately went out to wind her up.

Akash Give it a rest – you're beginning to sound like her.

Tara She always stood by us.

Akash She's dead, Tara. You don't have to re-invent her. I know. I was there. She was a crap mother. Locked you in your bedroom when you were revising for your A-levels, always pressurising, putting us down, nothing we did was ever good enough.

Priya looks upset.

Tara That's just not true.

Akash I'm telling you how it was.

Tara It's not how I remember it.

Akash I'm going to bed.

Akash walks out.
Tara turns back to the corpse and lovingly and carefully arranges the flowers around the coffin.

Priya They won't be able to cope without me.

Dilip They will learn to move on.

Priya I want to go back. Help me.

Dilip You can't go back. I keep telling you.

Priya Look, I know what's happening here. My body is just asleep and I need to find a way back in.

Dilip Your heart has stopped pumping.

Priya That's because I'm not in there.

Dilip Stop arguing! Listen to me.

Priya Why should I listen to you? I don't know who you are. Dressed up as my film idol. If I pulled away the mask, God only knows what I'd find underneath – eh? A monster? A wolf in sheep's clothing.

Dilip *You* called *me* yaar.

Priya I did not. (*Priya watches her daughter.*) She came back for me. She loved me. After our trip away, I was planning to go back to college – to finally finish my B.A. degree. I'd even started filling in the enrolment forms.

Dilip You've done that every year for . . .

Priya This year I was going to do it. You're dragging me away before I've done with it all. It should have been my decision – not yours.

Dilip I don't have the power over life and death. I am merely the guide.

Priya Then guide me back to where I want to go.

Dilip I can't.

Priya gets angry.

Priya You bastard.

Dilip Priya . . . let's not start all this again.

Priya You complete and utter shit. Standing around like a smug know-it-all. Telling me what I can and can't do.

Dilip Priya . . . you must let go. Pain, suffering, longing is all behind you now.

Priya Why don't you bugger off and leave me alone? I don't need you. I'll find my own way back.

Dilip (*annoyed*) Fine. I don't have to be here. I only go where I'm wanted.

Priya You're bloody not wanted here.

Dilip walks off in a huff – leaving Priya on her own. Priya walks over to the body and stands and stares at it.

This body served me well. We had some good times. Three babies came out – all wrinkled and soft – brand new. Such a clever body. Thighs spread and pushed them forwards, breasts fed them, arms held them, fingers and lips caressed their faces, eyes, looked and marvelled. Such a clever body. (*Priya shouts back at Dilip.*) You can't finish me off now. Not after everything I've been through.

Priya sits near the body and leans her head against the coffin.

SCENE THREE

It is morning. The body is still lying on the table and Priya has sat vigil all night.

Tara enters with yellow roses which she arranges on the body. She is dressed in a dark suit and looks very sombre.

Akash enters. He is also dressed in a dark suit. He doesn't even approach the body.

Akash The hearse is already here.

Priya looks worried.

Priya No, don't take me away.

Tara She's still wearing her wedding bangles. Are we supposed to take them off?

Akash I don't know. Where the hell's Baba?

Tara He's upstairs with Firoz Uncle.

Akash and Tara stand confused. Not knowing what to do next.

Tara It feels so unreal.

Akash Yeah. I suppose if this were India, we'd be parading through the streets with her on a stretcher. Her head jiggling around and us cheering all the way to the crematorium.

Tara Let's be thankful that we don't have to do that.

Akash The vultures are all out there, gagging to have a look at her. All queuing up in our drive.

Tara They're her friends, Akash.

Akash I wish they'd all just fuck off.

Firoz enters.

Akash Where's Baba?

Firoz He's not coming.

Akash What?

Firoz Don't worry, I'll be there. He says he can't bear to witness the fire.

Akash He doesn't have to, it all happens behind the scenes.

Firoz He's not in a good way.

Akash (*angry*) So? We're not exactly ecstatic. What are we supposed to tell all those people out there?

Firoz It doesn't matter what they think.

Akash This is ridiculous! I'm going to have a word with him.

Akash walks resolutely across the living room. Firoz catches him.

Firoz No. He can't face it Akash.

Tara Leave him.

Akash Doesn't he even want to say goodbye?

Firoz He's said his goodbyes. But he said that you have to . . .

Firoz produces a rough piece of wood and hands it to Akash. Akash looks at the piece of wood.

Akash I can't do this.

Tara Give it to me.

Tara takes the stick and Akash lights it. Tara and Akash walk towards the body with the stick in flames.

Firoz can't bear to look. He stands at some distance away.

Priya stands up. She is in a panic, desperate to stop them from lighting the flame on her.

Priya (*shouts*) Hey! Hey! What's going on? No! No! (*She rushes around to the body in the coffin and stands guard over it.*) Don't you dare. Keep that flame away from me. Please, please . . . (*She calls out.*) Dilip! Sahib! Where are you? (*Priya desperately looks around for Dilip.*) Where are you when I need you? They're trying to mutilate me. Murderers!

Akash and Tara walk around the body and eventually stand by Priya's dead body's head.

Dilip!

Dilip enters. He watches Priya.

Dilip Come on yaar.

Priya You've got to stop them.

Dilip approaches Priya and tries to pull her away gently. Priya however is not budging.

Dilip Please Priya, peaceful thoughts.

Priya (*to Dilip*) Get off.

Dilip You must move. You will affect the ritual.

Priya You're no bloody help. (*to Tara*) I'm trying to find a way to come back. Just a little more time.

Dilip There is an art to dying. Concentrate your energies now on the passage ahead. Meditate on the freedom your . . .

Priya Shut up you fool. Can't you see? They've given up on me.

Tara hesitates.

Tara Where does it have to go?

Firoz (*with his back to them*) In her mouth. Your father said that the flame has to touch her tongue.

Priya My tongue? You're going to burn my tongue?

Dilip Please Priya. This is not the way.

Priya Listen to me! Look, I'm here. I'm right here. Don't. Don't. Give me more time.

Dilip Priya – your time is up. Now come on yaar.

Dilip tries to pull Priya away now more forcefully. She struggles against him.
They tussle. In the ensuing struggle, Priya smacks Dilip hard on the jaw. He reels against the blow.
Tara places the flame in the mouth of the body. Akash and Firoz are both looking away. Priya screams and crumples to the ground holding her mouth.
Firoz and Akash then blow out all the candles and carry the body out. Tara follows them.
Priya is left on her own with Dilip. Dilip is nursing his jaw.

Priya What happens now?

Dilip They will return your body to the elements.

Priya Burn me.

Dilip You must be brave.

Priya That's all very well for you to say. That hurt.

Dilip Yes it did! But only because you struggled against it. Please, don't fight anymore. Soon, you will be free of all pain. You will be able to see more clearly and hear better. I have to say listening was never your strong point – so any improvement will obviously be a bonus.

Priya You can still be so flippant? Even at a time like this?

Dilip I am trying to make this easier – for both of us.

Priya I'm so cold.

Dilip reluctantly takes off his jacket and wraps it around Priya.
  Priya is suddenly afraid.

They've closed the lid, haven't they? Shut me in. Is this what it'll be like? Closed in a dark space?

Dilip No. It will be the opposite.

Priya There's someone else in here with me.

Dilip Someone else?

Priya She looks so frightened. Let her out. It's so dark.

Dilip It's just you.

Priya They're all outside.

We hear the sound of Shenai playing in the distance.

Dilip The funeral service.

We hear the sound of a priest chanting in Sanskrit.

Priya I'm really dead?

Dilip Yes, Priya, you are.

Priya shudders. She looks terrified.

Priya What will happen to me? I know you told me before, but I wasn't really listening. Can you get your notebook out again? Remind me? Please.

Dilip Priya, stay calm.

Priya Will you stay with me? You won't go away will you?

Dilip I am here.

Priya suddenly throws the coat off and starts to pace.

Priya I had so much more to do . . . to be snatched away like this . . . Will I be able to come back? Be reunited with them all in another life? Like you did in that film *Mehbooba*?

Dilip Ah now – that wasn't me.

Priya It was. You were in love with that court dancer – Nargis – wasn't it?

Dilip No, that was Hema Malini.

Priya Weren't you in that film?

Dilip Rajesh Khanna.

Priya I'm so hot.
What?

Dilip I didn't say anything.

Priya Don't leave me.

Dilip I'm here.

Priya groans with pain.

Priya You said it wouldn't hurt. (*She moans again.*) Feels like my belly's on fire. You said a power surge . . . this is just pain . . . I'm being squeezed and pushed. . . . Ohhh . . .

Priya pants and then lets out an almighty long scream and then collapses.

Dilip walks over to her and looks at her closely. He smiles.

We have some form of stage craft which signifies fire.

*It is later in the day. Tara drags in an old battered
suitcase. She looks around to make sure she is alone
before opening it. She hears her father approaching and
quickly hides the case.*

*Pradip enters with a large framed photo of Priya. He
looks around wondering where to put it.*

Pradip Your Mira Auntie brought this round.

Tara It's a nice picture of her. (*Tara looks around for an
appropriate space in the room.*) How about here?

*Tara helps her father to hang the picture. They both
stand back and look at it. Tara looks upset.*

*Pradip starts shuffling around the lounge tidying up
etc. He looks quite busy. Tara watches her father and
walks over to the mantelpiece where there is an urn of
ashes. She picks it up and examines it. Then she
watches her father.*

Tara You should have been there Baba – at the funeral.

Pradip does not answer.

Akash said it might be a good idea if we planted a rose
bush in the crematorium and scattered Ma's ashes there.

Pradip In the crematorium?

Tara Yes.

Pradip No, that would be too . . . depressing. Buried in
the soil? Surrounded by thorns?

Tara We'd have somewhere to go and visit her.

Pradip Like a grave?

Tara Are you hungry?

Pradip No.

Tara I could cook us some lunch.

Pradip I am not supposed to eat meat, though.

Tara How long for?

Pradip One month.

Tara looks at her father as if he is mad.

It is the custom!

Tara Baba – you're not even religious. What are you on?

Pradip These things must be done properly. In two days time, we must prepare all her favourite dishes and invite all her friends here to share our meal. It's like a send off for her soul to wish her luck on her journey ahead.

Tara Right.

Pradip If this is not done then the soul feels abandoned and lost.

Tara . . . So who's going to cook?

Pradip Your Amit Uncle will arrange it all. Where is Firoz?

Tara Still in bed. He was exhausted last night.

Pradip sits down, tired. Tara watches him warily.

I'm really glad he's here.

Pradip nods.

Pradip Where else would he be? I've known him longer than I can remember . . . and he was there the first time I ever clapped eyes on your mother.

Tara (*interested*) Yeah?

Pradip smiles at the memory.

Pradip It was during our final year at college. Firoz and I were walking along the canal bank when suddenly we saw this – this wild woman on her bike, flowers in her hair, sari hitched up and singing some film song at the top of her voice. We let her pass and she skidded to a halt. We stared. I mean she was quite a spectacle. She grinned at us both and asked, 'What are you gawking at?' We were speechless.

Tara So rude!

Pradip Then she salaamed us and rode away.

Tara giggles.

Tara I wish I could have seen her as she was then.

Pradip She had spirit. Stood out from her crowd of friends. Very bright. Like a sharp piece of glass.

Tara sits nearby and puts her arm around him.

(*hides his face*) Don't.

Tara Baba.

Pradip Don't.

Beat.

How long are you back for?

Tara I don't know. A month maybe.

Pradip Come back home. I hardly see you any more.

Tara But my work . . .

Pradip There must be other law firms in this country which deal with the same sort of things.

Tara Not as good as the one I'm with.

Pradip looks upset.

Pradip It would be nice to have my children around me now.

Tara I'll come and visit you more often.

Pradip What's going on in the boy-friend department?

Tara shrugs and smiles, embarrassed.

Tara Nothing . . .

Pradip I'm probably not long for this world either now. It would be so comforting to leave knowing that you at least were married . . . There's no one special?

Tara shakes her head

(*hopeful*) But there is someone?

Tara No – not really. (*Tara looks away, very uncomfortable.*)

Pradip Your mother was very proud of you.

Tara I know.

Beat.

Pradip But I want to see you settled.

Tara I am settled – I have an apartment in Paris which incidentally you hardly ever visit.

Pradip You're never there! Whenever I want to come and see you – you're off in some country with an unpronounceable name.

Tara Honestly!

Pradip Sometimes, I think you do it to avoid me.

Tara That's not fair.

Beat.

Pradip It's just the three of us now. You, me, Akash . . . we mustn't let the family disappear.

Tara It won't.

Pradip She was the one who held us together. Organised the birthdays, the parties – I left it all to her.

Tara Baba, we'll be fine. It'll take some getting used to but we'll muddle through.

Pradip I need to phone your Amit Uncle – sort out who we have to invite for the meal.

Tara Okay.

Pradip exits. Tara pulls out the old suitcase again, opens it and rumages around excitedly in the case. Akash enters. He startles her.

Akash What are you doing?

Tara looks guilty.

Akash Isn't that Ma's? The one she always said we weren't to touch.

Tara Yes.

Akash looks horrified.

Akash She'd kill you if . . .

Akash realises what he's saying and stops. He clocks the framed photo of Priya.
Tara gives her brother a sad look. He sits down, feet up on the table and lounging. He reads a newspaper.

Tara I've always wanted to know what she kept in this – haven't you?

Akash does not look up from the paper.

Akash Not really.

Tara ignores her brother and continues to rummage around. She produces a medal and reads the inscription on it.

Tara Awarded to Priya Das.All India General Knowledge Master – 1963. Jesus. Look – here's another one. (*Tara holds up another medal.*) 1964.

Akash She always did go on about how clever she was.

Tara picks out a beautiful peacock feather fan inlaid with silver. She opens it and closes it, fans herself and puts it down. On seeing it Akash picks it up and fingers it sadly. Tara then produces a battered old school satchel.

Tara I remember this. My first school satchel. Why did she keep this?

Akash To remind her of your genius.

Tara pulls out a wedding sari – old and slightly moth-eaten but still beautiful.

Tara Her wedding sari.

Then she pulls out a package, wrapped neatly in newspaper and tied up.

Akash What's that?

Tara and Akash handle the parcel mystified. Akash, despite his former misapprehension, fetches some scissors. Tara snips the string and opens the package carefully. Inside, there are small bundles wrapped in tissue.

It's like pass the parcel.

Tara opens the first one and pulls out a pink baby dress.

Tara That's so gross. Look at it. It's hardly surprising I turned out the way I did if this is how she dressed me.

Tara opens another package and another until they are surrounded by frilly, lacy hats, cardigans etc. All baby girl outfits. Akash watches with growing horror. He does not touch the outfits.

Akash (*angry*) Why does everything always have to revolve around you?

Tara What?

Akash Those outfits aren't yours.

Tara They're not yours, that's for sure.

Tara suddenly realises. She puts the dresses down in horror and looks at Akash.

Tara Oh my God. They're Chand's aren't they? All neatly wrapped – God.

Tara sits in awe for a moment and stares at the baby clothes.

Akash You know what she was like. Elephants never forget.

Tara Don't be so cruel.

Akash She's dead now. I can say what I like.

Tara Akash . . . imagine how she must have suffered. She lost a child! Don't you have any compassion?

Akash leaves, upset.
Tara looks at the baby clothes and looks after her brother.

Akash!

46

SCENE FIVE

It is now the afternoon. The room is filled with sunlight.

Dilip enters and starts pacing the room. Dilip keeps looking at his watch.
  We hear the sound of whispering.
  Priya enters the stage. She looks much younger and is dressed in a sari now. She looks fresh but bewildered.

Dilip How do you feel?

Priya Strange.

Dilip Good?

Priya (*incredulous*) Yes. I feel so light, so . . . like I'm floating and flying and . . . windborne.

Dilip Now, we have to get on. Two sunsets . . .

Priya What's all that noise? Like the buzzing of bees? Can you hear it?

Dilip We are in the realm of the newly dead. They are like you on their way to the waiting room.

Priya But what are they saying?

Dilip They are talking to their families.

Priya So sweet. Like humming birds. Wait . . .!

  Priya looks across the room and laughs.
  All through the next section, Priya and Dilip can hear and see things and respond correspondingly.

Dilip (*excited*) Can you see?

Priya Yes!

Dilip Excellent.

Priya Paddy fields outside my grandfather's house. Lush, green and my grandmother scolding me. I stole some sweetmeats from her shrine to Ganesh. I'm hiding behind my grandfather's rocking chair. He's protecting me. She is cursing me for stealing from the gods.

Dilip You always were a handful.

Priya And the stream down by the school, babbling over smooth rocks. I'm with father. We're throwing pebbles and he's lecturing me. I'm trying not to listen to him, concentrating on the sound of the water.

Dilip He's saying that you have to calm down. Stop being so wild otherwise no man will marry you.

Dilip and Priya laugh.

Priya Barely nine years old and already he's worrying!

Dilip What else can you see?

Priya So much. Everything, like shifting dreams. My mother taking me to see my first Dilip Kumar film – *Deedar*. She's weeping.

Dilip I have that effect on women.

Priya You've plucked out your own eyes and you're wandering aimlessly.

Dilip That was an early film. Melodrama was the catch-word in those days.

Priya Amit, my baby brother – suckling on my mother. I'm so jealous. I want to snatch him out from her arms and dash him to the ground. Look – there's my first admirer! Bhoglu, lolloping around like a baby hippo. (*She laughs.*)

Priya Can you see him?

Dilip Oh yes. Very handsome.

48

Priya The scent of the *rojoni gondho* flowers outside the house and coconut oil in my mother's hair . . . glass bangles tinkling as she washes me . . . I got into a fight with boys at school. They pushed me into a muddy pond. Mother is scrubbing me hard, her face tight. She is angry . . . It's moving, disappearing . . .

Dilip It will come in waves.

Priya Waves. That's what I can see. Emerald, grey and blue. Dark and swirling. I'm standing on deck feeling so clear and fresh. Just twenty-one. So young. Wondering what the future will hold. Will I always be this happy?

Dilip What about over there?

Priya looks.

Priya Pradip in his study, surrounded by books and dust . . . me trying to clean around him, angry, frustrated. So much hate . . . like poison in my belly. (*Priya looks away to another spot.*) There's me in the park with the children. Playing hide and seek. Akash is crying because he can't find me. Thinks I've left him, abandoned him in the dark, dark woods. 'Mummy, the bears will get me'. Let him cry a bit longer. Makes me feel needed. (*Priya moves across.*) The fishmongers. I'm buying some sea bream to cook. Firoz is coming to supper and I'm excited. I want the best. Then the noise, the crash, Akash screaming and screaming and screaming . . . (*Priya turns away suddenly and moans.*)

Dilip Priya – you must look.

Priya I can't.

Dilip You must.

Priya No.

Dilip It is important that you face your past.

Priya I don't want to.

Dilip shakes his head but looks resigned.

Dilip You know, you can enter mortal dreams.

Priya Can I speak to them?

Dilip Y–e–s . . .

Priya (*excited*) Show me! I want to speak to Tara.

Dilip Hold on yaar? I have to warn you. You can't just walk into a dream and have a normal conversation.

Priya You said I could talk to them.

Dilip Dreams are a complicated phenomenon. There are many different types. Of course there are the straight-forward wish fulfilment ones – yaar? Then there are the types where mortals simply remember incidents in their lives – Next are the completely nonsensical dreams: cows in the bathroom, people changing forms, out of space aliens sitting down for breakfast with you – that sort of thing.

Priya (*impatient*) But can I talk to them?

Dilip It's difficult. The dreamer controls the dream. You can't impose on them. It's a bit like walking underwater – whilst the dreamer has an advantage. They can move swiftly, changing directions, surprising you. You have to, quite simply, go with the flow.

Priya looks confused.

Dilip Basically Priya – you can't boss them around. It is their dream, not yours. Do you know who you want to talk to?

Priya Yes. Tara.

Dilip What, about Akash?

Priya No.

Dilip This is the last time you will be able to really talk to him.

Priya I don't know what to say to him.

Dilip Your attachment will start to fade around the third day as you start to leave everything behind.

Priya (*horrified*) You mean I'll forget them?

Dilip It will dissolve. A necessary part of the process if you are to go on.

Priya is upset.

Priya. Akash needs you.

Priya is thoughtful.

Priya Okay.

Dilip You need to stand firm and concentrate your energies. Look within you.

Priya Akash! (*Shouts.*) Akash! Wake up – it's me!

Nothing happens.

Is that it?

Dilip You're not doing it right. Focus your energies.

Priya (*softly*) Wake up, Akash.

Dilip No, no, no. You're just not entering into the spirit of things. Why do you make everything so complicated?

Priya I've never done this before.

Dilip I am trying to show you how to do this right. Then we can both get on. You're not supposed to be waking him up – you're trying to talk to him through his dreams. Enter his thoughts.

Priya How the hell am I supposed to do that? He can't see me, he can't touch me.

Dilip No, but you can reach him. Think of yourself as a sound wave, a flash of electricity You can go anywhere you want with him. Use your imagination, woman.

Priya concentrates hard.

That's it. That's more like it

Priya places her hand on her chest and closes her eyes.

Priya Akash.

As soon as his name is called, Akash enters. He sits down uncomfortably on a chair and looks around the room.

Akash You've changed the room around . . . again.

Priya is taken aback for a moment. She looks around her confused. (Dilip backs off but remains watching from the side.)

Priya Yes.

Akash Where's Baba?

Priya Erm . . .

Akash Don't tell me – he's upstairs marking exam papers.

Priya He'll be down in a bit.

Akash Smells good.

Priya Your favourite. Lamb curry.

Akash Great. Tara not here yet?

Priya Erm . . . no . . .

Priya turns and looks at Dilip, confused. He eggs her on. (Dilip backs off a bit more.)

You don't eat properly. You look pale. Does that girl-friend of yours know how to cook?

Akash Yes.

Priya Is she any good?

Akash Yeah. But I'm better anyway.

Priya (*laughs*) You? Cook?

Priya laughs a little too long and hard for Akash's liking.

Akash What's so funny?

Priya Sorry, it's just, you never . . .

Akash (*snaps*) Well I do now. (*He relents.*) Anyway, happy birthday.

He hands over a small package.

Priya For me?

Akash Yes.

Priya looks pleased.

Priya Can I open it now?

Akash 'Course.

Priya excitedly opens the package. It is the peacock feather fan. She opens the fan.
She doesn't look very happy though.

Priya It's . . . it's . . . beautiful.

Akash You don't like it.

Priya No – it's – it's just that peacock feathers are bad luck . . . the evil eye . . .

Akash looks away, hurt. Priya puts the fan away.

Still, it's the thought that counts. At least you didn't forget my birthday.

Akash I've never forgotten your birthday.

Priya So . . . you heard Tara's had a promotion?

Akash Yes. We celebrated when I went over a couple of weeks ago.

Priya You did?

Akash When's Baba going to finish?

Priya Soon.

They look awkward together. There is an embarrassed silence. Priya looks uncomfortable and at a loss as to what to say. She looks back to see where Dilip is but he has disappeared.

Any luck with the job-hunting?

Akash I have a job.

Priya I know but . . .

Akash It's all right, I earn enough, have a laugh, get to use the facilities.

Priya remains tight-lipped.

I know you don't approve of it – but being the assistant manager of a health club is actually quite a good job – almost respectable even by your standards.

Priya I only asked because you said to your father that you weren't happy there.

Beat.

Priya How's Tasleema?– we haven't seen her for a while. You should bring her with you next time.

Akash remains silent.

54

She's almost part of the family and you keep her away as if she's got the plague – or is it us you're ashamed of?

Akash Look, if you must know – Tasleema and I split up.

Priya (*shocked*) When?

Akash About six weeks ago – she's moved out to live with her mother.

Priya Why didn't you tell me?

Akash You never liked her.

Priya I didn't *dislike* her.

Akash just shakes his head.

What did you do to drive her away?

Akash I didn't do anything.

Priya That was it, wasn't it? You did nothing. I always said you took that girl for granted.

Akash You also said she was fat – to her face.

Priya I did not! I merely gave her the number of the local Weight Watchers club in your area.

Akash looks fed up.

I'm sorry . . . perhaps it was a bit insensitive. You should have said something.

Akash Yeah – like you always listen.

Priya What do you mean by that?

Akash Nothing.

Priya It's time you settled down Akash – you're always flitting from one girl-friend to the next.

Akash You want to arrange a marriage for me?

Priya Of course not. But if you treated your girl-friends with more love, more affection – perhaps they wouldn't always leave you.

Akash looks at his mother with hatred.

Akash I'm going to go up and see Baba. (*He gets up to leave.*)

Priya Please, Akash, sit and talk to me. We have so little time.

Akash pauses.

Priya I haven't seen you for weeks. You never sit and talk.

Akash What have I just been doing?

Priya Why are you always so angry?

Akash I'm not. It's you. You wind me up.

Priya looks hurt.

Priya (*shocked*) I'm your mother. How can you say such a thing?

Akash I'm just stating the truth.

Priya I've always loved you.

Akash (*dismissive*) Yeah – whatever.

Priya So ungrateful . . . (*Priya looks around her wildly.*) This isn't going to work – it's ridiculous. You never listened to me before – why should it be any different?

Akash Why won't you leave me alone? You're dead. You don't exist any more. And still, you haunt me when I'm asleep.

Priya All I ever wanted was for you to get on with life. You throw everything in my face after all the sacrifices I made?

Akash I was six years old when you sent me away.

Priya Don't bring this up now.

Akash You see, you're doing it again. You want to talk but not about the things that matter.

Priya What good will it do?

Akash That's it – pretend it never happened.

Priya Why are you being so cruel?

Akash You taught me. You pushed me away when I needed you most.

Priya Don't blame your inadequacies on me. I gave you life – but I won't take responsibility for your failures.

Akash If you were any sort of a mother – you'd take my failures as your own.

Priya Everyone's to blame except you? I came to this country with nothing . . .

Akash It isn't fair. Let me get on now. It's my life and you can't fuck me about any more.

Priya I made you. I brought you up. You owe me some respect.

Akash I don't owe you anything.

Priya Take, take, take. Sometimes you have to give back as well.

Akash (*menacing*) You want me to give back, do you?

Priya looks worried.

You are a selfish woman. You think about yourself and how things make you look. Obsessed with keeping up appearances. The nice clean house, the nuclear family, the curtains from John Lewis. Me and Tara are nothing

more than trophies. I don't know why you didn't shrink
our heads and put them on the mantelpiece for show.

Priya Stop it.

Akash Always ashamed of me. Always nagging and
scolding. So much dissatisfaction with your lot. Whining
and bemoaning your terrible fate. Landed with a third-
rate son. What did you do to deserve it? Karma! Eh?
Punished for sins in a past life.

Priya I never said that.

Akash Wished I was dead instead of Chand.

Priya Why are you saying such horrible things?

Akash You told me the night of the accident that you
wished it was me instead of her.

Priya I *never* said that.

Akash We all heard. Me, Tara, Baba. Don't try and deny
it.

Priya You're just making things up now.

Akash It's true. You said Chand was more precious to
you than me because she was made from love.

Priya You're lying. I was upset – my child had been
killed – but I never said those things. I don't know why
you're doing this to me.

Akash Admit it.

Priya I will not.

Akash Admit it!

Priya To make you feel better? No. You know what
your problem is? You never amounted to much because
of you and no one else. You failed your exams, got
sacked from jobs, failed in every relationship you ever

had because of you. You're unloved because you're so full of bitterness. Empty, shallow, stupid and vengeful. You walk around thinking the world and everyone in it owes you something. It's up to you. No one else.

Akash looks at Priya with hatred.

Akash I'm glad you're dead.

Akash exits. Priya watches after him, distraught. She half collapses in a chair and picks up the fan and looks at it.

Priya Bad luck.

Dilip, who has been standing in the shadows so far approaches her and puts his hand on her shoulder. Priya looks up at Dilip with pain.

That wasn't a dream, that was a nightmare.

Dilip Ah yes, I forgot to mention those ones.

Act Two

SCENE ONE

We are with Priya again. She is sitting in the same position as before, looking downcast and depressed.
  Dilip glides down from above, sporting a huge pair of black wings on his back.

Priya What's with the wings?

Dilip (*proud*) I saw it in a film once.

Priya A bit too symbolically Christian wouldn't you say?

Dilip Up there in the waiting room we simply exist. It's a great relief to free oneself from the shackles of the gods and prophets.

Priya Let's move on.

Dilip Move on where?

Priya Your waiting room.

Dilip But we've barely begun.

Priya Please. I can't . . . Akash hates me. He won't listen to me.

Dilip You have unfinished business.

Priya So you keep saying. But I don't know how I can finish it.

Dilip It's very simple. Unfinished business is merely a result of blocked communication. When we have been wounded, we often become defensive, always arguing from a position of being in the right . . .

Priya I have done nothing wrong.

Dilip . . . Blindly refusing to see the other person's point of view . . .

Priya You're beginning to bore me.

Dilip . . . This freezes the possibility of exchange.

Priya It's too late. Don't you see? I'm dead. Okay? I accept it. I've made my peace. Now let's get on with things.

Dilip (*irritated*) 'I've made my peace.' That's bollocks yaar.

Priya Are immortal souls supposed to say 'bollocks'? (*Priya looks longingly at Dilip.*) Tell me more about the waiting room.

Dilip What do you want to know?

Priya Is it a peaceful place? What's it like? Is it beautiful?

Dilip (*bored*) Oh yes, there are gardens and fountains . . .

Priya Really?

Dilip (*sarcastic*) . . . Rivers and valleys and lots of fat flying babies with cute little wings on their backs. Then they have all this smoke and mist around – it adds to the atmosphere. Mortals call it clouds.

Priya Come on . . .

Dilip Sometimes when you look up in the sky you can see the gods having chariot races. Vishnu versus Zeus – although Zeus is a terrible cheat . . . oh and the goddesses like a bit of mud wrestling. Durga always wrestles with Aphrodite – it's a long old rivalry between the two – but it's fun to watch. Durga obviously has an advantage because she's got ten arms . . . although it has to be said, Aphrodite's got a great body . . .

Priya You are making fun of me.

Dilip No. Me? Make fun of you?

Priya Let's go.

Dilip No.

Priya Please . . .

Dilip You are not ready. You're still in a period of transition and until you have found some peace of mind – your time in the waiting room will be spent in restless regrets.

Priya My only regret is that my son is useless. After all my hard work.

Dilip The hard work hasn't finished. Dying is much easier than being born. You brought him into the world.

Priya So it's all my fault? Even after everything I did? When I came to this country – we had nothing. No money, no connections . . .

Dilip yawns.

Dilip I know . . .

Priya Then you'll know how much I suffered. Pushed out, ridiculed, thousands of miles away from my land.

Dilip Still . . .

Priya My feet cracked with chilblains from the cold – hobbling around. Couldn't even afford to buy fish! I'd wait outside the fishmongers until the end of the day and wait for him to see me as he was throwing away all the fish heads and guts. I'd catch his eye and if he was in a good mood – he'd wrap them up in some newspaper and hand them to me.

Dilip They were hard times.

Priya (*smiles*) That fishmonger actually proposed to me. He came out one day, slightly shy, with the magnificent head of a twelve-pound salmon and said softly – 'If you married me love, you could have the head, the tail and all the body in between.'

Dilip You thought about it, though.

Priya Only for a moment. Then I'd go back and cook a fish curry – using frozen fish fingers to make up for the lack of flesh.

Dilip There's no doubting you struggled.

Priya I came to England with such hopes for myself. Freed from my parents. What did I do? I trapped myself in the octopus arms of another family. A family of my own making.

Dilip It's true – you gave a lot of yourself.

Priya So surely – I've earned a break? Take me to the waiting room.

Dilip shakes his head.
Priya looks down. Dilip puts his hand on her shoulder. Then, Priya hears the sound of waves.

(*excited*) I can hear the sea! Firoz!

Dilip He's dreaming about your boat journey together.

Firoz enters. His demeanour is different – less tired, younger.
Priya is excited and surprised to see him.

Firoz (*young, excited*) Can you hear the music? They're dancing down there. I just took a peek. It's like something out of an English fairy tale. The men are wearing suits and the women are all glittering with jewels. I saw the doctor and his wife in there as well. He was waddling around like a penguin. (*He laughs.*) You should have seen him. And she was dressed in her best *Benarasee* sari.

Priya Can we dance? Will you show me?

Firoz I can't.

Priya Why not?

Firoz I never learnt how to dance western style. I don't think a bit of *Kathak* fancy footwork would go down too well.

Priya You're useless.

Firoz Thank you. Anyway, it's all a load of rubbish. Indians aping the English and them feeling uncomfortable at having to be in the same room. Much better to be out here in the fresh air.

Priya If you hate the English so much why are you going to England?

Firoz I didn't say I hated the English.

Priya But you disapprove of them.

Firoz It's not them, it's the way that our people are around them which annoys me. So grateful to be taken on equal terms, so self-effacing. Don't you ever do that when you live there.

Priya Excuse me! Who do you think I am?

Firoz I'm just giving you some advice.

Priya Stop lecturing me.

Firoz It just annoys me. Have you noticed how that stupid doctor's wife looks down her nose at everyone? So superior. She insists on speaking to me in English – even though we could speak to each other in Hindi. And she has the nerve to go round diagnosing everyone's ailments. She's not the doctor – her husband is! She's probably not even a matriculate.

Priya (*teases*) Poor Firoz. It must be so hard for you.

Firoz What do you mean?

Priya Such a shame when you know that you're better than all of us put together.

Firoz makes a playful swipe at Priya who laughs and skips away.

(*continues to tease*) Firoz Khan, the great photographer. About to conquer the west with his prehistoric camera.

Firoz You wait, you'll see.

Priya I won't hold my breath.

Firoz What about you? What are you going to do when you get there?

Priya Learn to do the twist, cut my hair, wear miniskirts, smoke cigarettes and say 'cor blimey' every three seconds.

Firoz looks horrified and Priya laughs at his expression. Firoz shakes his head.

Firoz You love teasing me don't you?

Priya You make it s-o easy.

Firoz What will you really do?

Priya Enjoy my life.

Firoz No.

Priya You want me to be miserable?

Firoz Be serious, Priya. Pradip will be studying, working, and you haven't even thought about your future.

Priya You sound like my father. I'm not a child.

Firoz You're only twenty-one, completely green, never stepped outside Bengal let alone India.

Priya Please, don't patronise me.

Firoz England is an exciting place to be. My friends say there is so much work to do, money to make. You could finish off your degree – travel more. Get a swanky job in an office with an office boy.

Priya That would be something.

Firoz But you must make plans. That's what my grandfather always said. Take every opportunity thrown at you but always look one step ahead.

Priya It's better to be surprised by life, not to know what's around the corner. Don't you think?

Firoz But if you don't know what you want from life, how will you achieve anything?

Firoz looks at Priya.

Priya When I finish my degree, I'll teach, but now I've escaped from my family, Firoz. Let me have some fun.

Priya walks away from Firoz and looks out to sea. Firoz softens and approaches her.

Firoz (*gentle*) I want you to be happy.

Priya I will be. But I'm sick of people telling me what to do.

They both look out to sea.

Feel so at home here. I could almost live on the sea forever. Dive for pearls or become a pirate and bury my treasure on the bottom of the sea bed.

Firoz You're a couple of centuries too late.

Priya Maybe I'll start a new craze.

Beat.

Firoz We'll be landing in Egypt soon.

Priya When?

Firoz Two days apparently. It'll be nice to get some land under my feet. You'll have to stick close by. Pradip wouldn't thank me if some randy old Arab tried to snatch you for his harem.

Priya Might be quite exciting. Anyway, Arab women are supposed to be very beautiful. Liquid black eyes and fair skin. Maybe we'll find a wife for you there.

Priya laughs. Firoz watches her. He bends forward and kisses her tenderly on the cheek. Priya caresses his face and they embrace.

Firoz Why did you marry him? Why not me?

Priya You never asked.

Firoz looks bewildered. Priya looks lost. She turns back, her face to the sea. Firoz holds her from behind as the two continue to gaze out to sea. They look very comfortable together.

SCENE TWO

It is morning. Firoz is asleep on the couch. Pradip enters. He looks exhausted and is carrying two cups of coffee. He sits down on an armchair near the sleeping Firoz. He watches Firoz for a while and sips his coffee. Tara and Akash tiptoe in, still dressed in their night gear – carrying some croissants and things and placing them on the coffee table. They all sit down and watch Firoz.

Tara Doesn't he look sweet when he's asleep?

Eventually Firoz stretches and wakes.

Pradip Firoz Bhai – can't be very comfortable there.

Firoz No. It's not. (*Firoz sits up and looks around him slightly bewildered.*) What time is it?

Pradip About eight. I made you some coffee.

Tara And breakfast in bed. (*She pushes forward the croissants.*)

Firoz Thanks. I couldn't sleep last night, so I came down here to listen to some music. Must have fallen asleep on the couch.

Akash I slept badly too. Scared to shut my eyes.

Firoz Scared?

Akash Yeah. I kept saying over and over in my head, 'Now Ma – whatever you do, don't haunt me. I really could do without seeing you standing at the end of my bed.'

Firoz laughs.

Tara You wimp.

Firoz Understandable though. She would be a fearsome ghost.

Pradip One of those types that would pick you up by the scruff of the neck and shake you. 'Where's my whiskey! You've drunk all my whiskey!'

They all giggle at the thought.

Firoz I dreamt all night about the sea.

Pradip looks at Firoz, annoyed.

Tara I've been on the phone to work – there's been some emergency meeting called and I . . .

Pradip You must be here for the dinner, for your mother. We've invited all her friends and Amit is organising the food. It's important.

Tara I didn't mean I was going now . . .

Pradip Always such itchy feet, Tara. This is important.

Tara I'll be here.

Pradip (*to Firoz*) She can't stand still for a moment. Wants constant excitement . . .

Tara Hey! What is this?

Pradip Where to now? Eh? Outer Mongolia?

Tara Firoz Uncle! Come on – help me out here – you're my role model. Foot loose, fancy free.

Firoz It's not all it's cracked up to be.

Tara No responsibilities . . .

Firoz Listen Tara – you don't want to end up like me. It can be a long and lonely life.

> *Beat.*
>   *Tara and Akash exchange a glance.*

Tara I'd better get dressed. (*She exits.*)

Akash Me too . . . Baba, me and Tara are going out for the day.

Pradip Where are you going?

Akash Thought we'd head off to Hastings – where you and Ma used to take us?

> *Pradip stares ahead. Akash exchanges a look with Firoz and then approaches his father. He speaks to him gently.*

You okay?

Pradip No, not really.

Akash Why don't you come and stay with me for a while? Get out of this house? It'd be good for you.

Pradip Why don't you stay here? This is still your home.

Akash I've got to get back to work next week.

Pradip I'll be left here. An old man knocking around a big empty house. I'm finally on my own. The thing that I was always so scared of.

Akash (*snaps*) You're not on your own.

Pradip looks at Akash.

I'm sorry but honestly . . . We're both going to be around for you. And then there's Firoz Uncle.

Pradip looks depressed.

I know how it must feel. Everything's fallen apart . . .

Pradip You don't know how it feels. How could you?

Akash exits.
Pradip looks depressed.

Firoz You mustn't be so hard on them, Pradip. They've lost their mother . . .

Pradip Sometimes it feels like I'm the only one who cares.

Firoz You know that's not true.

Pradip (*relents*) Thanks for sticking around.

Firoz Come on . . .

Pradip I couldn't deal with all those people.

Firoz At least we'll have some respite for a while.

Pradip The phone hasn't stopped ringing and everyone wants details – 'How did it happen?' Like she tripped over and broke her arm. She's dead, what more can I say?

Firoz At least she was here, with you.

Pradip I was a coward. I couldn't bear going to the funeral.

Firoz Everyone understood.

Pradip But I should have gone. You did.

Firoz is silent.
  Pradip walks over to the mantelpiece and picks up the urn.

Pradip Her beautiful body reduced to this. Ashes.

Firoz Don't torture yourself, Pradip.

Pradip You know, one of the jobs I did as a teenager to pay for my school books was as an undertaker's assistant – cremating dead bodies.

Firoz I remember.

Pradip The fascinating thing about the way the body burns is that the hair is the first to go. It fizzles away with a hiss and a crackle. Quite gentle really . . .

Firoz Pradip please . . .

Pradip And you think the skin will just melt away nicely like the hair but then you notice it bubbling. You see the flesh and fat rising to the surface and then it starts to sizzle and spit like bacon on a grill. Suddenly there are hundreds of raw blisters that erupt on the body and . . .

Firoz (*shouts*) Stop it!

Beat.

Pradip I always assumed I would be the first to go. Women usually outlive their husbands, don't they? She never had any serious illnesses, no heart problems or the usual post-fifties diseases. She fell apart of course after Chand's death.

Firoz That was to be expected.

Pradip She wandered around for months in a kind of a daze. Even the children couldn't get through to her. I thought that she would die of a broken heart.

Firoz But she didn't.

Pradip No, but she was never the same. The sparkle went out of her eyes. Got obsessed with housework of all things. She never cared much for it before. She stopped wanting to be someone.

Firoz Not forever – surely?

Pradip Some of her old style came back but not all. I think it was me actually. In fact I know it was me. I irritated her.

Firoz How can you say that? She was devoted to you!

Pradip She was affectionate and caring and she looked after me like a mother cares for her child.

Firoz That's rubbish. I've never seen a more loyal wife.

Pradip looks at Firoz with amusement.

Pradip Why didn't you ever marry Firoz?

Firoz Let's not go through all that again. I'm too old now.

Pradip And too set in your ways.

Firoz There's that.

Pradip What happened to that rich Swiss woman you were hanging around with?

Firoz You know what happened.

Pradip She bought your studio for you and then you dumped her.

Firoz It was a mutual decision. We're still friends and she got her money back – eventually.

Pradip You should have married her instead of jet-setting around the world in search of the perfect photo.

Firoz I didn't love her. Anyway, I've had a good life.

Pradip Handed to you on a plate with a silver spoon. You never had to work to buy schoolbooks – just browsed in your grandfather's library.

Firoz What is this?

Pradip Even your work is about capturing other people's lives. You use them for your own glory.

Firoz I don't have to start defending my work to you.

Pradip All those women you photographed after the floods in Bangladesh – weeping and destroyed – did you ask them if you could step in and take their picture?

Firoz Pradip – don't start – because you're not exactly perfect. (*Firoz gets up to leave.*) I'll come back when you're in a better mood.

Pradip I always knew about you and Priya.

Firoz stops in his tracks. His back is turned to Pradip.

From the moment you stepped off that ship together. You walked away – didn't even greet me properly, and she looked so broken.

Firoz What are you raving about?

Firoz can't look at Pradip.

Pradip The funny thing is – I never, for a moment stopped loving her. I couldn't help myself. I tried for years to win her. Match fire with fire.

Beat.

We both fell in love with her on that day by the canal. But she *salaamed* you – not me. The Muslim greeting Firoz, not the Hindu one.

Firoz looks startled.

Firoz It was a long time ago. What's the point?

Pradip The point is – I always knew.

There is a long silence.

Firoz How can you be so . . . bloody noble? It's unnatural.

Beat.

Pradip Because she stayed with me and you never knew the joy of having children. I shared something with Priya that you could never have.

Firoz is quiet.

You never even knew Chand did you?

Firoz No.

Pradip I was surprised. Expected you to lay claim to her.

Firoz What?

Pradip You never showed any interest in seeing her. That's what amazed me. Sent a pink pair of booties from New York and that was it.

Firoz looks bewildered.

Firoz What are you saying?

Pradip Chand.

Firoz What about her?

Pradip She was yours and Priya's.

Firoz laughs, puzzled.

Firoz Pradip, what game are you playing?

Pradip You didn't know!

Firoz What are you talking about?

Pradip I thought you knew.

Firoz Chand was yours.

Pradip No. After Akash was born, Priya and I – she wouldn't let me near her and then suddenly she was pregnant.

Firoz looks around him wildly.

She told me herself. You were the father.

Firoz My daughter? Chand was my daughter?

Pradip Yes.

Firoz sits on the sofa. He looks lost and stunned.

Firoz She never said a word to me. Are you sure?

Pradip Oh – I'm sure all right.

Pradip watches Firoz's pain with relish.

You betrayed our friendship, not just once – but for years. This is your punishment.

Firoz You should have told me.

Pradip It was Priya who should have told you. Not me. Who was I? You ruined my family, my life. I was willing to take your child on as mine for her sake – not yours.

Firoz My child . . .?

Pradip As a result of Chand's death – I nearly lost Akash. He never got over it – all because of you.

Firoz I loved Priya.

Pradip She wasn't yours to love.

Firoz You didn't own her.

Pradip She was my wife.

Firoz Then you should have treated her better. You came to this country as equals but you betrayed her.

Pradip That's not true.

Firoz You were no different from her father. Never encouraged her to do anything with her life except wait on you hand on foot.

Pradip That's a lie.

Firoz I watched from the sidelines. Day in, day out, she waited for a word of encouragement from you. A little support, a gesture. But to you, she was just a woman. She would have showed you more love if only you had shown her some compassion.

Pradip She told you this?

Firoz She didn't have the courage to face up to you.

Pradip Priya was ferocious – everyone knows that.

Firoz Not when it came to herself. She wasted her mind, her talent, her education on your career – so that Pradip babu could be a respected academic in Britain.

Pradip You wanted to whisk her away from my 'tyranny'. Is that it?

Firoz I stood back because I knew you loved her. The first time I saw her, the elopement, the secret marriage, the journey over, the years of struggle when she tried to make a home with you. Even when I saw how you treated her. You were like a beggar who'd found a precious stone.

Pradip How dare you . . .!

Firoz I stood back even when I saw how you slowly eroded her self-confidence and turned her into a bloody housewife.

Pradip She was mine.

Firoz You see? Even now, you talk as if she was a piece of property. She was special.

Pradip She was my wife.

Firoz I know.

Pradip You still made love to her behind my back.

Firoz We stopped . . . after Chand's death . . . we never . . . ever . . . not again.

Pradip But you still yearned for each other. I saw it in your eyes, both of you, cuckolding me. You enjoyed it.

Firoz No, Pradip. We loved each other but the guilt was too much to bear for either of us.

Pradip Why didn't she leave me then? I wouldn't have stopped her.

Beat.

Firoz Because she loved you more, Pradip.

Firoz sits down, his energy spent. Pradip watches him.

All this time you knew? I had a daughter? I never even held her. Never saw her face . . .

Firoz sits for some time in tears. Pradip watches him with sympathy and sits close. As Firoz cries, Pradip takes his friend's hand in his. The two men sit together.
 Priya enters and stands stage right. She watches them both.

She looks downcast and miserable. Dilip is sitting up on a ledge high above her. He watches her as she enters. She looks up at him.

Priya (*angry*) I didn't want Firoz to find out like that.

Dilip It was bound to come out sooner or later.

Priya (*upset*) Why are you doing this to me?

Dilip I'm not doing anything. I have no control over them.

Priya He wasn't ever supposed to find out. Pradip and I agreed . . . what was the point? What a mess. (*Priya is distraught.*) It's torture. Showing me what a terrible person I was. How many people's lives I buggered up. And now I can't even put it right.

Dilip But they will. Now they have faced their demons and can move on.

Priya You sound more and more like a bloody shrink.

Priya looks at Pradip and Firoz.

D'you know – I had seen them both around the college. Always together they were like Laurel and Hardy. I must have walked past them with flowers in my hair at least ten times.

Dilip They never noticed you?

Priya Not even a backward glance.

Dilip Which one did you have a crush on?

Priya To be honest – both of them. So I decided to bugger up both their lives. Did a good job, didn't I?

Dilip Time is moving on.

Priya (*afraid*) Why do I have to witness all this? Are you trying to prepare me for the worst? Will I be punished?

Dilip Who by?

Priya Whoever's in charge up there.

Dilip What makes you assume someone's in charge?

Priya You must get your orders from someone.

Dilip Let's say we run as a collective.

Priya Will I go to hell?

Dilip is amused by this thought.

Priya For all I know, you might be *Saitan* – the devil himself.

Dilip (*bored*) This always comes up. Religion has such a brilliant way of scaring the living daylight out of mortals. How do you see hell?

Priya is thoughtful.

Priya Fire, torture, unremitting pain.

Dilip According to your religion there are twenty-eight different hells.

Priya Twenty-eight?

Dilip Didn't you know that? Of course it depends on your sin as to which one you go to.

Dilip takes out his notebook. As he reads out the descriptions of hell, Priya looks more and more horrified.

Tamsura is a region of darkness where *adulterers* are tortured . . . (*Dilip looks ostentatiously at Priya.*) *Liars* (*He looks at her again.*) go to *Raurava* where they are torn to pieces but not killed; those who have killed a Brahmin . . . have you killed a Brahmin?

Priya No!

Dilip That's okay, otherwise you have been fried in the fires of *Kalsutra*. *Krimibhoja* is a room where stubborn people having been transformed into worms will eat one another; those who have married outside their caste (that's you again, Priya) will be thrown into *Vajrakantaka* where they will be forced to embrace red hot statues. Arrogant people reside in *Suchimukha* where barbed wire is wound round their bodies and those who have caused disagreement amongst friends are thrown into *Vaitarani* river which is a stream of boiling urine, blood, shit, pus and other filthy liquids – though of course they do not die in it. Those who have given false testament . . .

Priya Please . . . I get the picture.

Dilip Of course, if you're a Jain – there are only seven hells, which is much more civilised. But they're even more graphic. Sinners get their nerves scraped, flesh torn and carved from their bones then minced in a grinder. Oh, this is a good one, then they rub chilli powder into your wounds.

Priya You've done your research haven't you?

Dilip I knew you'd ask. It's all rubbish of course.

Priya (*relieved*) Is it?

Dilip You don't believe all that nonsense – surely? It's not a test you have to pass. But one must learn from one's mistakes.

Priya Did I do anything right?

Dilip That's for you to decide. The only place hell really exists – is in here.

> *Dilip taps his forehead.*
> *Pradip and Firoz exit together. Priya watches them go. She is subdued.*

They are friends and they always will be. In their frail years to come – they will look after each other.

Akash and Tara are standing on the beach watching the waves. We hear seagulls and children in the distance. Akash has rolled up his trouser legs and is skimming pebbles.

Akash That was a beauty.

Tara tries to follow suit but fails.

No. You haven't got the wrist action. Look. First you have to find a flat pebble. Then you have to hook your forefinger round it like this . . .

Akash demonstrates, Tara copies him.

Arm back and then flick it – not up but across . . .

They both chuck their pebbles at the same time.

Excellent!

Tara Six bounces – that was better than yours.

Akash Beginner's luck.

Tara We'll see about that.

Tara skims another couple of pebbles and cheers her own efforts. They both laugh, clearly enjoying themselves. Then Tara stands back and savours the sea air.

It's nice to get out of there. Fresh air, sea breeze.

Akash The house is freaking me out. It's full of her. When I was shaving this morning I caught a sight of her reflection in my mirror, peering at me.

Tara doesn't say anything but looks at her brother with concern.

Tara I'm sorry – about those things I said. You know, the first night I got here.

Akash Forget it. You were upset.

Tara Didn't mean to take it out on you.

Beat.

Baba said you're going to cook for the big event.

Akash Yeah.

Tara Did you ever cook for her?

Akash Once. She complained that the fish was soggy.

Tara laughs.

The last time I saw her was four months ago on her birthday. Hardly spoke to her. Spent most of my time upstairs with Baba.

Tara I heard.

Akash She told you?

Tara Phoned me and bent my ear about how you ignored her. (*Tara starts to peer into rock pools and search for shells.*)

Akash We've got to try and get Baba out of that house, otherwise he'll just wallow around in misery.

Tara He always was good at wallowing. Remember the trouble Ma had getting him out of bed in the mornings?

Akash What about that time when she got you and me to pour a bucket of water over his head?

They both laugh.

Tara His face . . . she was so wicked.

Akash I thought she was going to let us do that to him every morning.

Tara If only.

Akash She used to screech like a banshee in the mornings like it was next to a world disaster if we didn't get up. The only time Tasleema stayed over, Ma frightened the living daylights out of her. (*He puts on a screechy voice.*) 'Ak–ash, Tas–lee–ma, Pra–dip! Breakfast!'

Tara laughs.

I'm seeing Tasleema next week, actually.

Tara Any chance of you two getting it back together?

Akash I don't know. I miss her but – I messed it up – treated her badly.

Tara Why?

Akash I don't know.

Tara What are you scared of?

Akash Being tied down.

Tara I never forget the way she stood on the table at Shukla's wedding and sang that song!

Akash She was completely legless.

Tara Yeah but she went up at least ten points in Ma's book.

Akash Did she?

Tara Oh yeah. Ma said she had spirit. Which means she approved.

Akash (*incredulous*) She liked Tasleema because she got slaughtered and stood on a table and sang a song?

Tara She liked Tasleema because she could see she made you happy . . . said she was a bit fat, though.

Akash can't help but laugh.

Akash What about Sophie?

Tara Fine.

Akash And?

Tara Wants us to live together – find a flat . . .

Akash And?

Tara I don't know if I'm ready.

Akash Three years and you're still not ready?

Tara I know. (*Tara stares out to sea.*) It's going to be so weird not having Ma around. I used to speak to her every week without fail. Sometimes, twice a week. She came to Paris loads of times, got on with all my friends, even Sophie, although of course, she didn't know – about us.

Akash You never told Ma?

Tara What was the point? She probably would have sent me to a psychiatrist or something. (*Tara looks guiltily at Akash.*) Anyway, some secrets are best kept.

Akash Are they?

Tara She always talked about you. How well you were doing, how handsome you were. She thought you were even more handsome than Dilip Kumar!

Akash hurls another pebble.

Akash She never talked to me the way she talked to you.

Tara (*sad*) I couldn't tell her the only thing that really mattered.

Beat.

Akash It would have been Chand's twenty-second birthday next week.

Tara instinctively links arms with Akash.

Tara Yeah.

Akash Fish and chips. Soaked in stinky vinegar and watery ketchup.

Tara Come on then.

Tara and Akash leave the beach arm in arm. As they exit, Priya stands for a moment, stage right, and watches them both go. She looks wistful. Then she exits.

SCENE FOUR

As Tara and Akash leave, Priya and Dilip enter. Priya is astounded by what she has just heard.

Priya (*mortified*) She never told me!

Dilip She had her reasons.

Priya I should have known.

Dilip You did all right by her.

Priya How can you say that? She should have been able to come to me instead of living this secret life. How awful for her – to have to lie to her parents.

Dilip We all hide something from our parents. It's natural.

Priya I was a terrible mother. I wasn't there for her. So busy pushing her to be something – I forgot to let her breathe.

Dilip But look at her, Priya. She is her own woman. She knows what she wants.

Priya My son hates me, Firoz must despise me and Pradip – poor Pradip thinks I never cared for him. And now . . . Tara . . . the one person I thought I understood – who I'd brought up well – she . . .

Priya is speechless.

Dilip Whatever you say, she loved and respected you and didn't want to hurt you.

Beat.

One more night. (*Dilip looks at Priya meaningfully.*) You will suffer if you go to the waiting room without facing your past. You gave Tara a good start. She will be fine. But Akash . . .

Priya He won't listen.

Dilip He's your son.

Priya I'm so tired.

Dilip You can't change the past. But you have the power to make him see.

Priya We always end up fighting.

Dilip (*urgent*) You must speak to him.

Beat.

Priya I don't think I can face another dream.

Dilip turns away.

If I could talk to him, face to face.

Dilip That's not possible.

Priya Surely I could appear . . .

Dilip Apparitions, ghostly visitations are strictly forbidden.

Priya By whom?

Dilip It's a rule. I could get into trouble. It frightens mortals. They get all worked up because they don't understand. Then they start screaming and it all gets horribly messy.

Priya So, he *can* see me?

Dilip realises that he's let the cat out of the bag.

Dilip (*admits*) He's already caught glimpses of you.

Priya Let me reveal myself to him properly.

Dilip It is beyond my powers.

Priya Surely rules can be broken?

Dilip Not this one.

Priya But you've seen what he's like. He's so stubborn!

Dilip (*sarcastic*) I wonder where he got that from?

Priya He will control the dream so that somehow I won't be able to say what I need to say.

Dilip He *is* hard work, I'll give you that.

Priya Please, Kumar *Ji,* let me approach him. You said yourself I'd suffer if I went on without speaking to him. Let me at least try . . .

Akash enters. He is carrying two large fish, a bunch of coriander, spices, bowls, knives etc. He comes and goes and lays the various things out on the table.
   Priya watches with interest. Akash lays the fish carefully out and gets busy, gutting the fish with a sharp knife.
   Priya looks at Dilip pleadingly.

He's my son. I want to speak to him – *properly.*

Dilip thinks for a moment.

Dilip Okay, okay, I'll give you five minutes. No bullying, no shouting and any screaming and you're out of there.

Priya Thank you. Thank you . . .

Dilip looks upwards with an apologetic air and then simply points at Priya.

Dilip Five minutes.

Akash looks up momentarily at his mother. He sees her and freezes.

Priya Please, don't be afraid.

Akash Go away. I can't see you. You're dead.

Priya I am here.

Akash I could really do without this.

Akash continues with his cooking.
Priya approaches him.

Priya You should have got the fishmonger to do that for you.

Akash This isn't happening. God rest your soul, rest in peace and all that . . . but please, just go away.

Priya peers greedily at the fish over Akash's shoulder.

Priya My favourite – sea bass. They look very fresh. How are you going to prepare that?

Akash Never you mind.

Priya You want me to help?

Akash (*incredulous*) No!

Priya I can grind the spices for you.

Beat.

Akash No.

Akash starts putting spices into a pestle and mortar. He grinds the spices.

Priya What's the occasion?

Akash You are.

Priya How many people?

Akash About fifty.

Priya Two fish for fifty people? Not enough fish. You need at least another five – and bigger ones.

Akash This isn't for everyone. This is for me, Tara, Baba and Uncle Firoz. Once everyone's fed and watered, we'll need to eat.

Priya Do you know what you're doing?

Akash ignores her and starts to scale the fish.

Make sure you rub in enough salt and *haldi* before you fry.

Akash Stop interfering.

Priya looks proudly at her son as he works.

Priya Akash, I want to show you something.

Akash I'm busy.

Priya Come on.

Akash I've got to get this ready.

We hear the whispering again.

Priya Can you hear?

Akash No.

Priya perseveres. She steps forward and looks around her. She can see things.

Priya I can see the past – so many things that we've forgotten. Come and have a look. (*Priya points to an imaginary spot.*) You have to focus otherwise it just looks like hazy clouds.

Akash looks up momentarily.

Akash I can't see anything.

Priya Look!

Akash stops what he is doing and looks up.

There you are. Five months old. So much hair, your first rice ceremony.

Akash shakes his head. Priya perseveres. She points in another direction.

There. You and Tara at the beach in Hastings.

Akash squints.

Akash What's she doing?

Priya Filling your swimming trunks with pebbles.

Akash You're laughing at me, Baba's scolding Tara.

Akash is hooked. He walks over to where Priya is and looks at another spot excitedly.

My first day at school.

Priya All those other children, bawling their eyes out and clinging to their mothers. But you look so brave and smart in your school uniform.

Akash You've just dumped me in the school hall and left me. But I won't cry.

Priya moves on.

Priya You and Tara are squeezed in bed between me and Baba.

Akash You jump up swearing at me because I've wet the bed.

Priya looks hurt.

Priya Over there. The pond we all dug out together in the back garden. You're feeding the tadpoles with a peanut butter sandwich.

Akash It's cold and you've locked me out of the house to punish me for something I broke.

Priya looks sad.

You've gone away somewhere and Dad's looking after us. He can't work out how to use the tin opener.

Priya Typical.

Akash So we dine on chocolate fingers and bread and butter. It's great fun. At bed time, Baba tells us ghost stories and acts them all out.

Beat.

I can see Chand. You've come back from 'somewhere' with her. You look happy and warm. Me and Tara stare and stare at her. We don't believe you when you say we were that small once.

Akash looks away. So does Priya.

I don't want to see any more.

Priya (*urges*) We must. We'll look together. (*She points with difficulty.*) Over there. Chand's crying and you're trying to cheer her up – rattling things and showing her your train set. Tara's got her hands over her ears, her nose in a book. She's no help. I am watching from the kitchen. I think you're so patient and gentle with her.

Akash She's standing up in her cot as I go in to see if she's woken up. She yelps when she sees me and calls out 'Atat'. She's trying to say my name!

Priya Her first word.

Akash And there, you're in the fishmonger's arguing over the prices.

Priya Firoz is coming to dinner tonight and I want to give him a special meal.

Akash You've left me outside with Chand in her push-chair.

Priya (*guilty*) I'm flirting with the fishmonger. Cajoling him to give me a good price.

Akash I'm in charge of Chand. She's crying. I wave at you through the window with the giant octopus painted on the front.

Priya I see you but I'm irritated. 'Just stay there! I'm nearly finished.'

Akash Tara sticks her tongue out at me. So I rock the pushchair. Still Chand cries, so I ease the brakes off and pretend we're in a train.

Priya You were always so good with her.

Akash I'm the engine driver. We go up and down the pavement 'choo–choo–choo–choo'. She's stopped crying.

Priya Tara's poking at one of the fish on display with her fingers. I slap her hand away.

Akash The train's picking up speed and I turn to hang out of the engine to wave at the passers by. Chand's laughing and waving too . . .

Priya One more stop to buy some onions . . .

Akash But then I push too hard and I lose my grip. The handle slips out of my hand and she rolls . . .

Priya Someone's shouting.

Akash I pushed her too hard!

Priya I hear a screech of tyres.

Akash I'm screaming and screaming, trying to catch the pushchair. But Chand's still laughing and waving as the car hits her.

Priya and Akash stop and watch the imaginary spot in horror.

Priya My baby.

Beat.

Akash After the accident – you sent me away to Amit Uncle's. A whole month! I didn't see you, or Tara, or Baba.

Priya We were just all confused. I was in a state of mourning. We brought you back.

Akash But you never spoke to me about it.

Priya It was too painful.

Akash What about me? Didn't you ever think how it would affect me?

Priya is quiet.

You never even let me go to the funeral to say goodbye.

Priya looks away.

I stole a photo of her from your album. You remember the one of the three of us sitting on the swing in our garden? Me between my two sisters. I hid it in my drawer – took it out to sleep with it under my pillow for a year and kissed it every night. You found it one day – remember? Almost a year after she had died. And what did you do?

Priya I can't remember.

Akash You took it away. I looked everywhere for it. You blamed me. You wanted to punish me.

Priya No.

Akash approaches Priya. He looks frightened.

Akash Maybe it wasn't an accident. That's what I keep thinking. I did it on purpose.

Priya is shocked.

Priya She was your sister. You adored her.

Akash I'm a murderer.

Priya (*distraught*) No! You mustn't believe that, if you do, you'll destroy yourself.

Akash But you left me in charge of her and I failed.

Priya You were only six years old.

Akash All this time, I knew I was guilty.

Priya It was an accident. I shouldn't have left you. It wasn't your fault.

Akash But she died and you hated me for that. You sent me away. All I ever wanted was for you to love me.

Priya I always loved you.

Akash You thought I was a failure.

Priya is distraught.

Priya *I* was the failure. Every year I sent off for the application forms to go back to university, to finish my degree. I never did it. I was desperate for you and Tara to succeed. Not to feel outcast and unworthy. I escaped, came here with so many dreams . . .

I didn't want you to make the same mistakes as me. My mother and father lived and died without ever uttering a word of comfort or affection to me. All their hopes and dreams were pinned on my brother. I was nothing. (*Priya looks at Akash closely.*) Terrible thing is – I turned into them. Treated you like they treated me. I never meant that to happen.

Akash looks at his mother with feeling. He starts to sob.

Akash And now – you're gone. And I'll never, ever see you again.

Priya watches as Akash cries. He cries like a child. Priya stands close.

Priya It's all right. It's all right. Shhh . . . I'm sorry, I'm sorry . . . Shhh . . .

Akash Will you see Chand?

Priya I hope so. Come . . . one last look. Come with me.

Priya takes Akash's hand and leads him forward. We hear the sound of children laughing. She points.

Can you see me?

Akash You're waiting outside my school. Looking out for me.

Priya Tara's gone to a friend's house. It's your ninth birthday and I have two huge ice creams dripping with chocolate sauce. It's a hot day and they are melting in my hand.

Akash I can see your face, your eyes. They soften when you see me. We eat the ice creams and you take me to Kew Gardens. We sit in the hothouse by the banana trees and you sing to me.

Priya holds Akash now and rocks him as if he were a baby. She sings as they break down together.

Dilip enters. He takes Priya gently by the arm and she leaves Akash reluctantly.
Akash is left on the stage on his own, crying.

SCENE FIVE

It is the final morning. The sun is out and the room is filled with light.
Firoz enters and stands before the large framed photo of Priya. It is now surrounded with garlands of flowers. He stares at the photo for a while before turning away, upset. Pradip enters.

Pradip That's the last of the guests gone.

Firoz Good. Anybody'd think they hadn't eaten for a month.

Pradip I think that all went off rather well.

Firoz The starving masses fed.

Pradip (*burbles*) Did you see how many chicken legs Jambu ate? I don't think his wife feeds him properly. Mind you . . . looks like she keeps it all for herself . . . Those mangoes were delicious.

Firoz Priya could polish off five mangoes in one sitting.

Pradip Five? More like ten.

Beat.

Sanjay did it again.

Firoz What's he said now?

Pradip Gave me his business card and said, 'You must come over to my office sometime and pop.'

Firoz Poor man – somebody really ought to send him back to school.

Pradip Akash's fish curry was excellent. Dare I say, just as good as Priya's.

Firoz It was good . . . where is he?

Pradip He and Tara went down the pub.

Firoz Oh.

Firoz is looking at Priya's picture on the wall again.

Pradip (*laughs sadly*) You wouldn't believe it but she was very drunk when that photo was taken. Cocktail party at Mira's. We were all swimming in rum.

Firoz and Pradip sit in silence for a moment.

I was thinking of going with Amit to India – to the Ganges, to take Priya's ashes back.

Pradip looks at Firoz.

Firoz Me?

Pradip Why not?

Firoz What about Tara and Akash? Why don't you take them?

Pradip They say they have to get back to work. Come with me. It'll be our last farewell to Priya.

Firoz I've said my farewells at the funeral. It's your turn now.

Pradip nods understanding.

Pradip Akash goes home tomorrow – Tara next week and you . . .?

Firoz I'll get off tonight. I have things to do . . .

Pradip Of course –

Firoz (*tentative*) Will you manage?

Pradip I have to, Firoz bhai – what choice do I have?

Firoz gets up.

Firoz I'll call in on the pub on my way. Fancy a drink?

Pradip Hmmm? No – you go.

*Firoz pats Pradip affectionately on the back and exits.
As he leaves, he passes Priya, who enters. She looks
after Firoz for a moment and then moves across to sit
close to Pradip. Pradip sits alone, looking lost. He
gets up and pours himself some whiskey. He looks at
the empty bottle.*

The last of Priya's precious whiskey.

*Pradip looks around the room, lonely, and sits down
again. He stares ahead of him sadly.
    Priya affectionately caresses Pradip's hair as Pradip
closes his eyes. Husband and wife sit together for a
while in a strange kind of harmony.
    Dilip now enters stage right, carrying a picnic
basket. He lays out a little table cloth on the floor and
produces a plate of strawberries from the basket. He
arranges the strawberries with care on a plate. Then
he produces a bottle and two glasses and pours two
drinks. We hear birdsong and see sunshine.
    Dilip sits and waits. He steals a strawberry guiltily
and munches it. Priya watches him curiously and
eventually is drawn away from Pradip's side.*

Priya What's this in aid of?

Dilip A little celebration.

Dilip hands Priya a glass.

Priya Champagne.

Dilip No. It's my own concoction.

Priya eyes the drink suspiciously.

Much better than champagne.

Dilip raises his glass as Pradip does at the same time.

Pradip A toast to Priya . . . Long may your soul be free.

Priya raises her glass to Pradip and then takes a sip.

Priya Hmmm . . . excellent!

She gulps back the drink as does Pradip, who then exits.
   Dilip offers the plate of strawberries to Priya.

Priya I would have preferred mangoes.

Dilip But these have the outward beauty of a strawberry and the inside perfection of a mango.

Priya nibbles at one.

Priya (*incredulous*) Delicious!

Dilip So, almost there.

Priya looks back sadly.

Any regrets?

Priya Only several thousand.

Dilip laughs and pours Priya out some more drink.

It's hard to put right a whole lifetime of mistakes in three days.

Priya gulps back her drink.

Dilip You did all right. And it wasn't a lifetime of mistakes.

Priya points at the strawberries.

Priya Can I have another one?

Dilip They're for you, Priya. Have as many as you like.

Priya Thank you.

Priya takes a few. She starts to giggle.

Dilip (*amused*) What?

Priya I was thinking of that awful film you did with Raj Kapoor.

Priya starts to sing one of the hit songs from Andaz.

Dilip Don't remind me.

Priya gets up and dances whilst Dilip continues with the song. They sing and dance in true Hindi film style – they enjoy themselves.

So, Priya. It's almost time. You feeling okay to leave this all behind?

Priya I'm not sure that I did much good.

Dilip You set Akash back on the right path . . . eventually.

Priya Only in death.

Dilip Even so . . .

Priya I was a housewife. An educated one – but still a housewife. I cooked, I cleaned, I made up rules, no shoes to be worn in the house and no phone calls after midnight. Not exactly a great offering to humanity.

Dilip You are too hard on yourself.

Priya My death leaves very little behind.

Dilip Your soul will merge with the universal *atman* but will still remain an individual ready to be reborn.

Priya looks confused
Dilip looks at Priya for a while.

Nothing can die because everything leaves a residue and every residue is a beginning. There is an old parable in your religion which I quite like. They get it all wrong when they talk about *karma* of course but the story of the *atman* is more true.

The father gives his son a nut and asks him, 'What's in this nut?'

The son says, 'In the nut, is the kernel.'

The father asks 'What is in the kernel?'

The son says, 'In essence: the nut tree which one day may grow out of it.'

The father then asks, 'And what is there even deeper in the nut?'

'The essence of life which causes the fertilisation of all things.'

'And what is there inside that?'

When the son has no reply, the father says '*Tat tuam asi:* that is you.'

Priya Do you know, that's the most profound thing you've said in all the time we've been together?

Dilip Don't look so surprised.

Priya Is that a line from one of your films?

Dilip No it isn't!

It is windy and blustery now. Dilip stands and faces the wind. He puts on his shades and places his overcoat across Priya's shoulders. Priya looks anxious.

Come. It'll be all right.

He helps Priya to her feet. Priya takes another gulp of the 'champagne' and takes the plate of strawberries with her.

Priya This waiting room, I hope it's not going to be like a doctor's surgery.

Dilip Don't be ridiculous.

Priya Lots of dead people sitting around coughing, with their legs in bandages and stuff.

Dilip You are the most idiotic of women.

As they argue, a very bright light engulfs them gradually.

Priya I'm only asking!

Dilip If you'd listened to me in the first place instead of trying to constantly shout me down.

Priya It's not fair. Can't you read out from your notebook again?

Dilip No.

Priya Go on.

Dilip We don't have the time.

Priya walks into the light. We see her sillouhette as she begins to disappear.

Priya (*ecstatic*) My goodness! It's so beautiful.

Dilip listens with a knowing pleasure as Priya's excitement grows.

I could pluck fistfuls of it and put it in my pockets . . . I know. I know! And the children . . . Look at the children!

The light dissolves and Priya's laughter dissolves until it is just a distant echo.
Dilip stands on his own, breathes a sigh of relief and consults his notebook.

Dilip So . . . Who do I have to be now?

His face drops.

No! Ugh . . . Elvis Presley?

Dilip exits the stage muttering under his breath.

Why can't I get people like Mahatma Gandhi or Che Guevara? Elvis Buggery Presley?

The light fades on Priya's photo.
End.